WOMEN
IN HISTORY

WOMEN AND LITERATURE

Veronica Doubleday

WOMEN
IN HISTORY

Women and Business
Women and Education
Women and Literature
Women and Politics
Women in Science and Medicine
Women and Sport
Women and the Arts
Women and the Family
Women and War
Women and Work

Series editor: Amanda Earl
Consultants: Pauline M. Young MA, Dip Ed,
  Senior Lecturer in English and Theatre Studies
  at The Polytechnic of Wales
Designer: Joyce Chester
Picture Editors: Jane Marrow and Liz Miller

Front cover: Edith Sitwell (1888–1964), writer and poet, painted by Wyndham Lewis in 1923 (completed 1935).
Back cover: Top left – Mary Wollstonecraft (1759–97), pioneer feminist and writer. Top right – Harriet Martineau (1802–76), leading journalist, social commentator and popular writer on economics. Bottom left – Vita Sackville-West (1892–1962), distinguished novelist, poet and critic. Bottom right – Anita Desai (b. 1937), contemporary novelist and children's writer on life in India.

First published in 1988 by
Wayland (Publishers) Limited
61 Western Road, Hove
East Sussex, BN3 1JD, England

©Copyright 1988 Wayland (Publishers) Limited

British Library Cataloguing in Publication Data
Doubleday, Veronica
  Women and literature – (Women in history).
  1. English literature. Women writers,
  1660–1988 – Critical studies
  I. Title   II. Series
  820.9'9287

ISBN 1 85210 389 2

Typeset by Butler & Tanner Ltd
Printed and bound in Great Britain by
Butler & Tanner Ltd, Frome and London

Picture acknowledgements
The pictures in this book were supplied by the following: Aldus Archive 4 (below), 9, 14, 28; Barnaby's Picture Library 41; BBC Hulton Picture Library back cover (top right), 4 (above), 11, 12, 22, 23 (left), 26 (below), 27 (right), 33, 35 (left), 37, 43 (above), 44 (below); The Bridgeman Art Library 36 (above); The Fawcett Library 35 (right); Girton College Archives 29 (below); John Frost Historical Newspapers 31 (right); The Lords Gallery 31 (left); The Mansell Collection back cover (top left and bottom left), 20 (below), 21, 23 (right); Mary Evans Picture Library 7, 8 (both), 13 (The Fawcett Library), 15 (above), 18 (below), 19, 20 (above), 25, 26 (above), 27 (left), 38 (The Fawcett Library/Spare Rib); Mills and Boon (Publishers) Limited 36 (below); Penguin Books back cover (bottom right); Picturepoint 29 (above); Rex Features 43 (below); Topham 6, 34, 42; Virago Press 32. The remaining pictures are from the Wayland Picture Library.

Permissions
The publisher would like to thank the following for allowing certain extracts to be used in the book: The estate of Virginia Woolf and The Hogarth Press for *The Waves* by Virginia Woolf. Faber and Faber Limited for *The Bell Jar* by Sylvia Plath. Grafton Books for *The Female Eunuch* by Germaine Greer. Michael Joseph Limited for *The Golden Notebook* by Doris Lessing. Victor Gollancz Limited for *Testament of Youth* by Vera Brittain. Virago Press for *The Diaries of Hannah Cullwick* and Princeton University Press for *A Literature of Their Own* by Elaine Showalter.

The publishers would like to thank The Tate Gallery, Omar S. Pound and the estate of Mrs G. A. Wyndham Lewis for allowing us permission to reproduce Wyndham Lewis's painting of Edith Sitwell on the front cover of the book. The publishers would also like to thank The British Museum and The Fawcett Library for the use of the early monthly magazine covers, and Leila Boakes for her help with the text.

Contents

1

Introduction – 'scribbling women'

George Eliot, one of the most outstanding novelists in English literature, was encouraged to write by her partner.

Below *Virginia Woolf believed that a woman needed economic independence and peace and quiet in order to write.*

The subject of women and literature is vast. In this book we will be looking mainly at its history in Britain, although American and European writers who have been particularly influential are also included.

In 1928, the novelist Virginia Woolf (1882–1941) gave some famous lectures at Cambridge University about the history of women's writing called *A Room of One's Own*. She asked her audience to imagine the story of Shakespeare's brilliant sister: could she have become a successful writer? For a start she was not sent to school, but had to sneak books from her brother. Then, her father engaged her to be married, so she ran away to London, where she was alone and vulnerable. Eventually a theatre manager took an interest in her, but she became pregnant and eventually committed suicide... The story illustrated the huge difference in the lives of men and women. Given equal talent, Shakespeare's sister would probably never have become a famous writer – simply because she was a woman.

What made it so difficult for women to write and to have their work appreciated?

• Up until the nineteenth century many people thought it improper or 'unladylike' for women to make a name for themselves. It was hard for women to publish their work, and very often doing so endangered their own or their family's reputation.

• Because of this, women often published anonymously or took pseudonyms (pen-names). This meant that their work was not recognized as their own. Much women's writing has been neglected or forgotten.

• In general, girls' education has been inferior to boys. People did not think it was useful for girls to read books and gain knowledge. For a long period, girls were not taught Latin or Greek, yet knowledge of the Classics was considered essential for writers. Consequently women had less confidence in writing than men, and far less encouragement.

• Critics, historians and publishers in the past have almost always been male, as have teachers in the famous public schools for boys, and many have treated women's work unfairly. Often they

ridiculed or dismissed it simply because it was by a woman. Sometimes they made personal remarks about the author's looks or morals, rather than judge her work.

● Women have been limited in what they could write about. For centuries they were excluded from the public world of law, science, government and politics: their experience was confined to family, friends and home. What is more, some subjects were felt to be 'unsuitable' for ladies to write about.

● Women, especially of the working classes, had family commitments and often had no time to concentrate on writing.

Why is women's writing important? Too often the male view of the world has been accepted as the only one. Women can give a female point of view which is interesting and valuable.

Above left Until the mid-nineteenth century, most girls did not go to school, but learned 'feminine' skills such as sewing and graceful manners at home.

Above In contrast, most boys of the upper classes were taught many academic subjects at school.

Certain themes run through women's writing:
- Marriage has had a very different meaning for women. For centuries it was the only 'career' open to women, and was vital for their economic support.
- Women have written with great sympathy about people who are powerless or poor — such as slaves or factory workers. This is because as women they, too, were often the underdogs.
- Men have often glorified war, whereas women have more generally seen it in terms of suffering and waste.
- Women have written perceptively about female friendships, whereas male writers have usually viewed women only in relation to men.

A very important theme in women's writing is protest about their inferior position in society. Their work has often been filled with frustration and resentment. Virginia Woolf felt that this anger served to hamper the woman writer. 'Her books will be deformed and twisted. She will write in a rage when she should write calmly ... She is at war with her lot.'

Much of women's writing has been forgotten because it was not published or valued when it was written. Yet it means a great deal to women to have their own tradition to look back on. Sometimes modern authors refer to an earlier work by a woman and produce extraordinary results — as when Jean Rhys wrote *Wide Sargasso Sea* (1966). This follows the life of Mrs Rochester, the mad woman in Charlotte Brontë's *Jane Eyre* (1845).

Women in the past who did have the determination to write and became successful as writers, despite the many obstacles, often fell into certain categories.
- Many were unmarried — such as Jane Austen and Emily Brontë.
- Many were childless — such as Virginia Woolf and Charlotte Brontë (who only married towards the end of her life).
- Some had husbands or partners who encouraged their work, including Elizabeth Gaskell and George Eliot.
- Some had fathers who encouraged their work — such as Fanny Burney and Maria Edgeworth. (Mothers and sisters were usually powerless to provide economic support, and so appeared less significant).
- Some women writers, however, were overshadowed by more famous brothers, including William Wordsworth's sister Dorothy and Henry Fielding's sister Sarah (a respected and famous novelist in her time, but now almost forgotten).

Virginia Woolf came to the conclusion that the woman writer needed peace and economic independence: 'A woman must have money and a room of her own if she is to write fiction'.

Virginia Woolf's beautifully hand-painted writing desk, and spectacles.

2

Literary Beginnings

1660-1750

Until the seventeenth century women played little part in the writing, production or distribution of books or other printed matter. From the seventeenth century onwards, women writers began to have work published, and to be paid for their writing – two very big steps in establishing women in the world of literature.

There were many reasons why women did not write or publish; the most basic factor was education. Women, and men, from the lower classes did not go to school and could not read or write. Even if such women had been able to read, their household and agricultural work left them no free time for books. Although aristocratic and middle-class girls were taught to read and write, few were given any 'classical' training in Greek and Latin. Knowledge of great writers such as Homer and Virgil and their poetic styles was felt to be essential for any writer.

In those days most middle-class women stayed at home and did not play much part in public life – they were not expected to attend business meetings or official functions, for instance. Most people believed that women had their own 'feminine sphere' of activity related to the family and the home, while men controlled the public domain. Women who rebelled against this idea were accused of being 'unfeminine'. Socially they were restricted to their neighbours and relatives. Men regularly gathered in coffee-houses and talked about news, books and gossip, but women had no public meeting places to discuss their experiences or ideas. Believe it or not, it was even socially unacceptable for women to go into bookshops and look at books – for it was feared they might learn something unsuitable or shocking!

Often it was impossible for women to find any quiet time at home to think and write. Some upper-class ladies used their leisure time for writing poetry, essays and translations, which they sent round to their friends, but it was unthinkable for them to publish: that would be unladylike. The first women who dared to go into print had to be prepared to put up with violent criticism and to be called names such as 'petticoat authors' or 'scribbling women'.

Margaret Cavendish, Duchess of Newcastle (1623–73) protested

Above *Margaret Cavendish was an eccentric seventeenth-century writer, whose nickname was 'Mad Madge'.*

'
I, a woman, cannot be exempt from the malice and aspersions of spiteful tongues, which they cast upon my poor writings...
Margaret Cavendish, *Epistle to her husband*, 1667.
'

'
Alas, A woman that attempts the pen,
Such an intruder on the rights of men,
Anne Finch, mid-seventeenth century.
'

Above In the seventeenth and eighteenth century, men often met in coffee houses to discuss ideas. It was not 'suitable' for women to be seen in such places.

Below The poet Katherine Philips.

against the custom of keeping women in the background. 'All I desire is fame', she wrote. She was nicknamed 'Mad Madge', partly because she was so keen to be recognized as a writer. She was very eccentric and liked inventing her own original fashions for publicity. On her rare visits to London she was surrounded by huge crowds of staring, tittering people. The diarist Samuel Pepys waited to see her pass and caught a glimpse of her in a velvet cap with her long loose hair all round her, riding in a silver coach with footmen dressed in velvet. She wrote a great many books – poetry, plays, essays – and spoke out for women's right to be equal to men, particularly in education. She insisted that women should not 'live like bats or owls, labour like beasts and die like worms'.

By contrast, the poet Katherine Philips (1631–64) made every effort to avoid publicity. She had no desire to be an outcast from society because she was a writer, and she firmly refused to publish. Her work was highly praised among her literary friends, and she established an important group of writers – including several famous male poets – who met regularly at her house, following the French 'salon' (drawing room) tradition. They all adopted flowery pseudonyms; her own was 'Orinda'. Shortly before her death in a London smallpox epidemic, a collection of her poems was published without her permission. She was embarrassed and furious and declared that she had 'never written a line in my life with the intention of having it printed'. The book was withdrawn, and her collected poems appeared only after her death. Her translation of the French tragedy *Pompey*, produced in 1663, is notable for being the first work by an Englishwoman to be performed on the stage.

Aphra Behn (1640–89) was one of the first women in Britain to write for a living, competing successfully on equal terms with men. She was particularly famous as a writer of clever, entertaining plays and had at least seventeen staged during her lifetime.

Towards the end of the seventeenth century, magazines for women began to appear, opening up new possibilities for female writers: the *Athenian Mercury* in 1690 was followed by the *Ladies' Mercury* in 1693. These periodicals, containing some news, sketches and a section on personal problems rather like an 'agony column', were popular with women from aristocratic and middle-class families. In 1709 *The Tatler* appeared; it was published three times a week to catch the country mail coaches, and appealed to women from the growing middle class.

Mary de la Rivière Manley (1663–1724) was a journalist and successful writer of poems, plays, novels and satires (essays which criticized famous people through scorn or ridicule). She was tricked into marriage when very young, and was pregnant when her husband

From a mother complaining about her fourteen-year-old daughter, who **thinks of nothing but going to the publick breakfastings at Ranelagh with her friends, and again in the evening, and what shall she wear...** Eliza Haywood sympathized with the mother, but warned her against being too strict. *Female Spectator*, 1744.

During the eighteenth century, aristocratic and middle-class families had plenty of leisure time. Ladies' magazines became increasingly popular.

Below The Female Spectator was a popular magazine that was later published in book form.

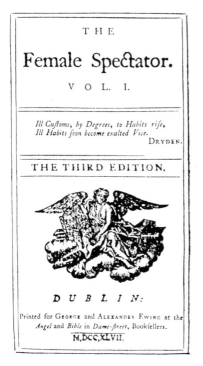

THE

Female Spectator.

V O L. I.

Ill Customs, by Degrees, to Habits rise,
Ill Habits soon become exalted Vice.
                                        DRYDEN.

THE THIRD EDITION.

D U B L I N:

Printed for GEORGE and ALEXANDER EWING at the
Angel and *Bible* in *Dame-street*, Booksellers.
M,DCC,XLVII.

later deserted her. Somehow Manley had to find a way to support herself. Difficult circumstances often forced early female authors into the writing profession.

At that time the public loved gossip and Manley saw that she could make money by writing 'scandals' about well-known people. In any case, she believed it was good for the public to know the truth. In 1705 she wrote *The Secret History of Queen Zarah*, which told of the adultery, cheating and bribery of aristocrats and politicians in a thinly-disguised story. She even gave a 'key' listing the real names of those involved. The book was an instant success. Her most famous and outrageous work, *The New Atlantis*, appeared in 1709. She was arrested and charged with damaging people's reputations, but managed to escape prison.

In addition, Manley made a serious contribution to women's journalism, and in 1709 brought out a new magazine called the *Female Tatler*. She worked with Jonathan Swift (author of *Gulliver's Travels*) on a weekly newspaper, *The Examiner*, and took over its editorship from him in 1711. Swift said he was too frightened to walk home through the eastern part of London at night, but Manley jumped at the opportunity to take on his job!

Eliza Haywood (1693–1756) wrote for almost forty years. She and Aphra Behn were early novelists, but historians have overlooked their work and claimed Daniel Defoe and Samuel Richardson as the 'fathers' of the English novel. Eliza Haywood wrote at least 67 works: novels, 'scandals' like Manley's, histories, plays and translations. She also worked as a journalist, most memorably in her monthly essay-paper, *Female Spectator* (1744–6) which was later collected into bound volumes. Her novels reflect the changing mood of the time, away from a relatively liberal outlook and towards greater respectability. Her first, *Love in Excess* (1719), was sensational; a much later, equally successful work, *The History of Miss Betsy Thoughtless* (1751) was more moralistic. *Love in Excess* was, with Swift's *Gulliver's Travels* and Defoe's *Robinson Crusoe*, one of the three most popular works of fiction before Samuel Richardson published his first novel in 1740.

It is typical of the history of women writers, however, that Eliza Haywood is more often remembered for the gossip surrounding her private life than for her work. She was parted from her husband and apparently had two illegitimate children, facts which her rivals used against her. Swift called her 'that infamous scribbling female' and the poet Alexander Pope attacked her spitefully in his satire, *The Dunciad*.

The first professional women writers worked hard to support themselves, and were frequently short of money. They suffered insults and criticism, but established their independence and a place in the literary world.

Aphra Behn (1640–89)

Aphra Behn came from a middle-class background and became a widow at a young age. At that time, a woman without male support had few options. Teaching and spinning were very poorly paid, and being an actress or courtesan (high-class prostitute) was very disreputable. Rather than remarry, Behn decided to support herself by writing and became a very successful playwright, poet and novelist. She was the first woman ever to make a living in this way.

As a reaction to the grim period of Civil War (1642–1646) and the strict Puritan rule, the public wanted immoral, bawdy entertainments. She outdid her male rivals in writing lively comedies about sex and politics, but from a new female point of view, and boldly spoke out for women's right to enjoy love. Her first play, *The Forced Marriage*, was performed in 1670, and her greatest success was *The Rover* (1677). She also wrote thirteen novels and collections of poems, including state poems to commemorate important events.

At the end of her life, times in Britain were troubled and the theatres did poorly, so she took to writing novels. Her important early contribution in this field has been sadly neglected. Her most famous novel, *Oroonoko* (1688), has never lost popularity: a horrifying account of slavery in Surinam (Dutch Guiana), which she visited as a young woman. In it she describes the white settlers as 'notorious villains', 'more brutish by far than the very heathens themselves'. All her sympathy is with the African slaves. *Oroonoko* was the first attack on slavery in English literature, and the first English novel with a black hero. It later became very important for campaigners against slavery.

Aphra Behn was the first woman to earn her living by writing plays for the theatre.

Aphra Behn was hard-working, but often short of money. In 1666 she went to Holland to spy for King Charles II. He did not pay her expenses for this work, so she was sent to a debtors' prison for a short while. During her career she suffered much criticism as a woman intruding into the male literary world. Although she had many famous and influential friends, including the writer John Dryden, she was often viciously attacked and called names like 'that lewd harlot'. After her death, times became more prudish and her open treatment of sex made her work too shocking to be read. 'If Mrs Behn is read at all, it can only be from a love of impurity for its own sake, for rank indecency ...', a critic wrote in the *Saturday Review* in 1862.

Further reading: *Reconstructing Aphra*, Angeline Goreau (Oxford University Press, 1980).

3

Education and Reform

1690-1800

Above *An early charity school.*

6 ▬▬▬▬▬▬▬

'How was you educated?'
'At a boarding-school.'
'After what manner?'
'By the help of a French dancing master, a French singing master and a French waiting woman. Before I could speak plain English, I was taught to jabber French . . .' The Ladies' Catechism (a pamplet attacking girls' education), 1703.

▬▬▬▬▬▬▬**,**

By the beginning of the eighteenth century, girls' education was still inadequate. More schools existed, but there was no systematic training of teachers and educational standards varied a great deal. At girls' charity schools (for the poor or orphaned) far more time was spent on handicrafts than academic work. Wealthier families educated their daughters at home, or sent them to boarding schools where they learned 'social graces' — such as elegant French phrases to drop into conversation at dinner parties — but very little serious knowledge. In general, education reflected class: poor girls were destined for work, richer girls to be idle, pretty ornaments.

An important critic of the system was Mary Astell (1668–1731), the daughter of a Newcastle merchant. In her *Serious Proposal* (1694) she urged women to have greater expectations in life. She believed ignorance and a narrow education had a long-lasting 'evil' influence. She proposed the foundation of a female residential college, like a 'monastery', where women could escape from everyday pressures and be trained as teachers. Her idea met with enthusiasm and a wealthy lady promised £10,000 for the college, a great deal of money at the time. However, a bishop misunderstood the word 'monastery', thought it might be a Roman Catholic plot and put a stop to the scheme! Daniel Defoe (author of *Robinson Crusoe*) supported her ideas in *The Education of Women* (1697), but another century and a half passed before a women's college was founded.

A group of ladies called the bluestockings did a great deal to prove that women could hold their own as scholars. (Interestingly, the term 'bluestocking' — first given because a male visitor to the group wore informal blue stockings rather than 'full dress' black silk stockings — has now been turned into a name for a woman who is thought too 'bookish' and therefore dowdy and humourless.) Elizabeth Carter (1717–1806) was the most learned of the group. Her father taught her Latin, Greek and Hebrew; a French refugee taught her French, and she taught herself Italian, Spanish, German, Arabic and Portuguese. She also studied astronomy and the geography of ancient history. At sixteen Elizabeth Carter contributed verse to the *Gentleman's Magazine* and continued to publish poetry and

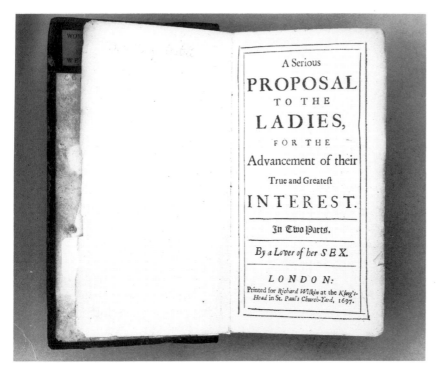

An original copy of Mary Astell's Serious Proposal, first published in 1694. Her ideas about founding a woman's educational college were far ahead of their time.

translations – sometimes for large sums of money. The bluestockings often met at the London house of Elizabeth Montagu, whom the author Dr Johnson called 'the Queen of the Blues'. They were joined by important men such as the painter Joshua Reynolds and Dr Johnson himself. Fanny Burney (1752–1840), who became famous for her novels and diaries, was a younger member of their set.

The French Revolution of 1789 inspired some British people to argue for educational and social reform. One of the most outstanding was Mary Wollstonecraft (1759–97), who went to Paris to witness events for herself. She was very original and free-thinking in her ideas. Her influential book, *Vindication of the Rights of Woman* (1792), argued convincingly that women had as much creative potential as men, and should be allowed to use it. She challenged existing ideas about a woman's proper place in society and explained how women were trapped into dependence on men. Having been a school teacher and governess herself, she was also concerned about the absence of education for girls, and supported the ideas of another author, Catherine Macaulay (1731–91), whose *Letters on Education* had appeared in 1790. (This book had been paid a very back-handed compliment by the *Gentleman's Magazine* – 'Mrs Macaulay's work is really wonderful considering her sex'!) Unfortunately, Mary Wollstonecraft's life was cut short: she died at thirty-six after giving birth to a daughter, Mary, who later became author of the well-known Gothic novel *Frankenstein* (1818).

❛
Let your children be brought up together, let their sports and studies be the same ... the wisdom of your daughters will preserve them from the bane of coquetry ... Your sons will look for something more solid in women than a mere outside ...
Catherine Macaulay, *Letters on Education*, 1790.
❜

Right *Mary Wollstonecraft was inspired by the events of the French Revolution. She went to Paris and saw ordinary people protesting about the unjust way their country was run. Her famous book,* Vindication of the Rights of Woman, *described the unfair position of women in society.*

6

Independence I have long considered as the grand blessing of life, the basis of every virtue . . . Mary Wollstonecraft, *Vindication of the Rights of Woman,* 1792.

9

6

It is a singular injustice which is often exercized towards women, first to give them a very defective education, and then to expect from them the most undeviating purity of conduct. Hannah More, *Strictures on the Modern System of Female Education,* 1799.

9

Another woman who worked to raise educational standards was Hannah More (1745–1833), although she strongly disapproved of Mary Wollstonecraft and her revolutionary friends. She refused to read the *Vindication* because she herself believed in 'subordination' — that women should accept a lower status than men. Hannah More was a friend of the actor David Garrick and wrote for the stage. Her tragedy *Percy* was performed at Covent Garden in 1777.

More was a member of the bluestockings and was very serious-minded. Some people rudely called her 'the She-Bishop in petticoats' because she had a rather preaching manner. With her sisters she started an excellent girls' school in Bristol. Her *Strictures on the Modern System of Female Education* (1799) called for improved standards and had a widespread influence, but she was careful not to threaten men's status and warned against women becoming too 'puffed up with the conceit of talents as to neglect the plain duties of life'.

More had a genuine concern for the poor. (By now some poor people had learned to read and write at charity schools.) When she investigated the reading matter that was available to them — broadsheets sold by street pedlars — she was shocked by their bloodthirsty and superstitious nature, and by the revolutionary message that some carried. She copied the broadsheet format and used similar woodcut prints to illustrate simple, entertaining stories which aimed 'to attack gross immorality or dishonest practice'. Between the years 1795–8 she published over a hundred different *Cheap Repository Tracts*, as these broadsheets were called. Three thousand were sold in three weeks, and within a year sales reached two million. Bound volumes for wealthier people also sold well. At the end of her life she and her sisters retired to Somerset and set up Sunday schools for the poor, and industrial schools for girls to learn spinning.

There was growing need for suitable educational books and stories. Maria Edgeworth (1767–1849), the second surviving child in a family of twenty-two children, went to live in Ireland in 1782. Her father (who was married four times) was deeply interested in education and their household functioned as an experimental school. Father and daughter worked together and kept detailed records of the children's progress. *Practical Education* (1798) was the result of their observations

Above Hannah More, an important educational reformer. Her Cheap Repository Tracts *were simple stories for the poor, and sold in their millions.*

and experiments, and it had a great impact in Britain and France. Edgeworth's *Early Lessons* appeared in 1801, and her *Harry and Lucy* stories were the first planned reading scheme for young children. She had the great advantage of being able to test her work on her brothers and sisters. She went on to become a much admired and well-known novelist, whose stories were lively but always instructive. They include *Castle Rackrent* (1800), about Irish life, and *Belinda* (1801), which was admired by Jane Austen.

Left Maria Edgeworth at her desk in the family library in Ireland. She was one of the first people to write educational stories for children.

❛
A woman, especially, if she have the misfortune of knowing anything, should conceal it as well as she can. Jane Austen, *Persuasion,* 1818.
❜

A label from a Minerva Library book. Note the request to return the book promptly!

4

Female Novelists

1770-1820

By the middle of the eighteenth century there was a growing fashion among women for reading novels. Novelists had begun writing books 'suitable' for ladies and young girls, which did not contain language or scenes that were immoral or explicit. Also the growing numbers of middle-class women had more leisure time because they had servants to help them. This gave them more time to entertain themselves.

Books had also become more easily obtainable. In about 1770, the publisher William Lane opened the Minerva Circulating Library to promote fiction for women from the Minerva Press. His library began in London, but soon expanded to fashionable towns such as Bath, Cheltenham and Brighton. For the first time middle- and lower-middle-class women could hire as many books as they could read for a small annual subscription. Girls read more, and domestic servants joined the fashion, finding that novels relieved the boredom of their long hours on call.

The expanded market for books was a great benefit to female authors. In fact, more novels were published by women than by men: some men took to writing Minerva Press romances under female pseudonyms! However, many people looked down on these novels as time-wasting nonsense; they had a rather 'low-brow' image — partly because they were associated with women. They were not all frothy love stories: some were clever and original, breaking new ground in style and subject matter.

As we have seen before, many women became authors because they fell on hard times and needed money. Charlotte Smith (1749–1806) was married at fifteen to a spendthrift who was continually in debt. Eventually she left him — a daring thing to do in those days — and supported their eight children by writing. She preferred writing poetry, but had to concentrate on novels because they paid better. Her best-known book, *The Old Manor House* (1793), is set during the American War of Independence. She brought political ideas into her stories, which were true to life and did not always end happily.

Fanny Burney (1752–1840) became famous for her novels, diaries and letters. Her first novel *Evelina* (1778), published anonymously,

> **I know not a more pitiable case. Chained to her desk like a slave to his oar, with no other means of subsistence for herself and her numerous children . . . she is indeed to be pitied . . .** William Cowper (1731–1800), the poet, on Charlotte Smith.

was an immediate success. It was an amusing, observant account of a young girl's entrance into society. Later she wrote in her own name and became a member of the witty and learned bluestocking set [see Chapter 3]. *Cecilia* (1782) brought her the inconvenient honour of being made Second Keeper of the Robes to Queen Charlotte. Had she been a man she could have been rewarded with a university or diplomatic post, but this royal appointment virtually stopped her from writing novels. After five years she begged to leave the court, and married a penniless French refugee. A later novel, *Camilla* (1796), made her more than £2,000: she bought a house in the country and called it 'Camilla Cottage'.

Some novels achieved spectacular success. An outstanding example was *The Mysteries of Udolpho* by Ann Radcliffe (1764–1823), which appeared in 1794 at the height of a great fashion for 'Gothic' novels.

6

In the first place, you must not cough. If you find a cough tickling in your throat, you must arrest it from making any sound; if you find yourself choking in the forbearance, you must choke but not cough . . . Directions for coughing, sneezing, or moving, before the King and Queen, Fanny Burney's diaries.

9

Right An illustration from Ann Radcliffe's The Mysteries of Udolpho. It was one of the most famous 'Gothic' novels of the time.

6

The hollow moan struck upon Emily's heart, and served to render more gloomy and terrific every object around her – the mountains shaded in twilight – the gleaming torrent, hoarsely roaring – the black forest and the deep glen . . . Ann Radcliffe, *The Mysteries of Udolpho*, 1794.

9

6

Catherine's heart beat quick, but her courage did not fail her. With a cheek flushed by hope, and an eye straining with curiosity, her fingers grasped the handle of the drawer and drew it forth. It was entirely empty . . . Jane Austen, *Northanger Abbey*, 1818.

9

Above A title page from La Belle
Assemblée, 1807. *This was one of the
many fashionable periodicals of the
period.*

Below Jane Austen, one of the most
important writers in English literature.

The Gothic style relied on exotic locations, suspense and a spine-chilling atmosphere — all designed to make the hair stand on end! Ann Radcliffe wrote several other novels and was popular well into the Victorian period. Her work was translated into French and Italian and writers such as Byron, Keats, Coleridge and Scott were all influenced by her. Jane Austen made fun of Gothic novels in *Northanger Abbey* (1818): her naive heroine Catherine Morland avidly reads *The Mysteries of Udolpho*, continually imagining similar horrors and mysteries in her own life.

Jane Austen (1775–1817), undoubtedly the best-known and most highly regarded author of this period, admired many of the female novelists of her time, including Fanny Burney, Charlotte Smith and Maria Edgeworth. When she started work on *Mansfield Park* she joked that she wanted to imitate — and improve on — a novel she found extremely clever: *Self Control* by Mary Brunton (1778–1818). In the story of *Mansfield Park* Jane Austen also included an amateur performance of *Lovers' Vows*, a popular romantic comedy adapted from a German play by Elizabeth Inchbald. Embarrassing and unlady-like love scenes in the play pose a moral problem for Austen's characters, and the heroine resolutely refuses to take part in the performance.

Austen, the daughter of a Hampshire clergyman, began writing for her family, whom she described as 'great novel readers and not ashamed of being so'. Before the age of seventeen she had written many sketches, short comedies and mock-serious tales, and at twenty she finished an early version of *Sense and Sensibility*. At first she published anonymously, but by 1814 her name was known. In the following year she dedicated *Emma* to the Prince Regent, a great admirer of her work. Her novels, brilliantly clever and ironical descriptions of social manners, are among the best in the English language. Many of them champion the cause for serious education for women, instead of piano-playing, sewing and singing.

Around the turn of the century another set of bluestockings gathered in London. Some wrote poetry; others worked as editors of fashionable magazines such as *Keepsake* and *La Belle Assemblée*. Several wrote 'silver fork' novels, so called because they depicted high society life. One of the most lively authors of such novels was Sydney Owenson (1783–1859), who became Lady Morgan. She was born in Dublin, the daughter of an actor and theatre manager who was often very poor. Before her writing success she worked as a governess. Hardly more than four feet tall, she was clever, witty and much in demand at parties. *The Wild Irish Girl* (1806) made her reputation as a writer. She was the first woman writer to receive a literary pension: £300 a year 'in acknowledgement of the services rendered by her to the world of letters'.

Elizabeth Inchbald (1753–1821)

Elizabeth Inchbald was born in Suffolk, the youngest in a large Catholic family. Determined to lead an independent life, she ran away from home to become an actress. Eventually, she married a much older actor. They toured Britain and France on the stage together but had continual financial problems. She worried a lot about losing her looks and, when her husband died, she decided that play writing might earn more money than acting. Her first successful play, *The Mogul's Tale*, was staged in 1784, and in 1787 she received the handsome sum of £900 for *Such Things Are*. By 1789 she had given up acting and become a well-established playwright.

Inchbald was a leading authority on drama and wrote theatre criticism for *The Artist* and *The Edinburgh Review* magazines. In 1805 the publisher Longman invited her to edit and write prefaces for his twenty-five volume *The British Theatre*. She had to provide a short biography of each playwright and an assessment of the plays. One author took offence at her criticism and sent an angry letter written in sarcastic, flowery language. '... those dramas of mine which have already had the honour to be somewhat singed, in passing the fiery ordeal of feminine fingers...' Although she wrote a witty reply, the experience upset her and she refused later offers to write critical reviews, no matter how hard publishers and editors coaxed her.

Novels did not pay as well as plays, but Elizabeth Inchbald wrote two, of which *A Simple Story* (published in 1791, but begun in 1777) was highly praised. Maria Edgeworth wrote to tell her how impressed she was by its realism. Towards the end of Inchbald's life she was so famous that a publisher offered £1,000 for her memoirs without even seeing the manuscript.

Further reading: *Mothers of the Novel*, Dale Spender (Pandora, 1986).

Act V. LADY JANE GRAY. *Scene last.*

De Wilde pinxt. *Audinet sculp.*

M.rs INCHBALD as LADY JANE GRAY.

In dear remembrance of thy love, I leave thee
This book, the law of everlasting truth.

London, Printed for J Bell British Library, Strand Nov.r 26. 1791.

Elizabeth Inchbald was an actress before she became a successful playwright and drama critic. This picture shows her playing Lady Jane Grey, who was Queen of England for ten days but executed in 1554.

Charlotte Brontë. She first published her books under a man's name, hoping to be judged more fairly.

❛ *[In Victorian reviews] we find that women writers were acknowledged to possess sentiment, refinement, tact, observation . . . and knowledge of the female character . . . Male writers had most of the desirable qualities: power . . . clarity, learning . . . shrewdness, experience, humour, knowledge of everyone's character, and open-mindedness.* Elaine Showalter, *A Literature of Their Own*, 1977. **❜**

5

The Early Victorian Era

1820-1860

Writers such as Fanny Burney, Maria Edgeworth and Jane Austen established the novel as a form in which women could excel. Nevertheless, it was not always easy for women to publish; there was still an atmosphere of disapproval. This may have been due to the fact that 'sentimental' and 'mass market' novels were often produced by women. 'Serious' novels, with the exception of a notable few, were still thought to be the domain of men. Many women began writing anonymously; others took male pseudonyms so as to have a hidden identity.

In 1846 Charlotte Brontë (1816–55) and her sisters, Emily and Anne, published their poems under the names Currer, Ellis and Acton Bell. The book did not receive much notice, but in the following year Charlotte's novel *Jane Eyre* (again published under the name Currer Bell), caused a sensation. Some critics guessed it was by a woman, but were baffled because it had such 'masculine' power. They argued fiercely about whether Currer Bell was male or female, using sections of the text as 'proof'. Readers were shocked because the heroine, a plain governess, expressed passionate feelings for her employer.

Right *Charlotte, Emily and Anne Brontë with their brother Branwell. The sisters were dedicated writers and each became famous in her own right.*

Many hostile reviews were by women, offended at any hint of female sexuality, and the novel was labelled 'sensual', 'gross' and 'animal'. Charlotte Brontë was upset and amazed that her expression of emotion — which now seems utterly tame — should be thought so improper.

Adopting male pseudonyms did not stop women from being assessed by a different standard from men. Before passing judgment, critics would guess whether an author was male or female (not always accurately — sometimes they made embarrassing errors!). Then they would assume there were certain weaknesses in women's writing and claim the most important skills for men. In 1849 Charlotte Brontë wrote to an influential critic: 'I wish you did not think me a woman. I wish all reviewers believed 'Currer Bell' to be a man: they would be more just to him.'

Women novelists began to rebel against the idea that they should be limited to 'feminine' subjects. They wanted freedom to write about many issues — from politics to philosophy. Many began exploring social issues from a new female viewpoint. In *Jane Eyre* and *Shirley* (1849) Charlotte Brontë described the fate of spinsters and governesses, criticizing the lack of opportunities for women outside marriage. Elizabeth Gaskell wrote about social injustice and inequality. George Eliot (whose real name was Marian Evans) raised moral questions about human relationships and society. There was also a significant shift from upper-class to middle- or working-class settings.

An important inspiration for such changes came from the French novelist and playwright George Sand (1804–76), a socialist and influential political figure. She spoke out for women's freedom of expression and outraged society by openly taking lovers, smoking cigars and sometimes wearing men's clothes. Her work was greatly admired in Britain, and the poet Elizabeth Barrett Browning wrote a sonnet in praise of her genius, and George Eliot took the name 'George' in her honour.

In 1856 George Eliot (1819–80), the unpaid editor of *The Westminster Review*, had some stories published in *Blackwood's Magazine* and began writing fiction at the suggestion of the writer and critic G. H. Lewes, who had already encouraged Charlotte Brontë and others. George Eliot and Lewes lived together but could not marry as he was separated, though not divorced, from his wife. For several years George Eliot was cut off from 'polite' society for 'living in sin'. Despite this she became the most highly revered woman author of her time. *Middlemarch* (1871–2), a study of country life, was judged her masterpiece. In her last novel *Daniel Deronda* (1876) she examined anti-Semitism and the hidden world of the Jews, and created a remarkable heroine, Gwendolin Harleth, who married for power, not for love.

> ' *... probably I shall be an old maid. I shall live to see Robert married to someone else ... I shall never marry. What was I created for, I wonder? Where is my place in the world?* Charlotte Brontë, *Shirley*, 1849. '

The French novelist George Sand influenced many British women writers.

Elizabeth Gaskell (1810–65) was one of the first novelists to write about working-class people. She lived in Manchester and was married to a senior church minister. Both Gaskell and her husband were very active in helping the poor. In 1839–41 the city was hit by a 'cotton famine' (because the imported cotton crop failed) and there was no work in the mills. Gaskell witnessed great hardship. Soon afterwards she lost a baby son and became so depressed that her husband encouraged her to write. Her first novel *Mary Barton* (1848) was published anonymously. It caused a great outcry and resulted in many angry letters being sent to the local papers. In it she revealed the selfishness of factory owners and showed the horrors of industrial life. A later novel, *Ruth* (1853), told the sad story of a woman who was seduced and had an illegitimate child. Many people felt this was an immoral subject and members of Elizabeth Gaskell's church publicly burnt the book. The fact that she was a highly respectable wife and mother helped her stand up to her critics – whereas Charlotte Brontë was often cruelly branded as a frustrated, ugly spinster.

More women now began working in other branches of writing, especially journalism. Geraldine Jewsbury (1812–80), a novelist and critic, selected and rejected work at the big publishing house of Bentleys. Harriet Martineau (1802–76) was an important newspaper journalist and writer on social problems.

The novel remained the most 'acceptable' form for women writers.

Victims of the cotton famine in Manchester in 1839 queue for food. Elizabeth Gaskell's novels were among the first to portray the hardship of working-class life.

It was harder to succeed as a poet. The Brontë sisters first published as poets, but made their name as novelists. From childhood they had composed private romantic sagas set in the imaginary lands of Gondal and Angria. Emily Brontë (1818–48) became famous for the unique *Wuthering Heights* (1847), generally considered among the greatest English novels. However her remarkable poetry, which she regarded as intensely private and saw published with extreme reluctance, went virtually unnoticed.

A woman who did succeed as a public poet was Elizabeth Barrett Browning (1806–61), who was so well known that when Wordsworth died she was almost made poet laureate. For some years she lived in her father's house as a bed-ridden invalid, writing and studying. Then she ran away to Italy with the poet Robert Browning, who considered her work of greater value than his own. The story of their romantic marriage became famous, but meant that later she was chiefly admired for her love poems, *Sonnets from the Portuguese* (1845). Male critics could accept her image as a loving wife while they greeted with hostility *Aurora Leigh* (1856–7), her famous 'novel-poem' about a woman writer. This was a passionate plea for women's liberation and Elizabeth Barrett Browning felt it was her most important work: 'I mean that when you have read my new book, you put away all my other poems ... and know me only by the new'. Despite the critics' reaction it was enthusiastically received by the public.

Below The poet Christina Rossetti. Her work was full of personal feeling, and often reflected her very religious lifestyle.

Above Elizabeth Barrett Browning with her favourite pet spaniel, Flush.

'
We must not look at Goblin men,
We must not buy their fruits;
Who knows upon what soil they
*   fed*
Their hungry thirsty roots?
Christina Rossetti, *Goblin Market*,
1862.
'

'
I was soon surrounded by strange
men, who examined and
handled me in the same manner
that a butcher would a calf . . . I
was then put up for sale. The
bidding commenced at a few
pounds . . . I then saw my sisters
led forth, and sold to different
owners . . . When the sale was
over, my mother hugged and
kissed us and mourned over
us . . . Mary Prince, *The History of*
Mary Prince, a West Indian Slave,
1831.
'

Christina Rossetti (1830–94), the daughter of an Italian political refugee, was another notable poet. Her first work was printed privately when she was only twelve. Her brother, Dante Gabriel Rossetti, was a gifted painter who helped form the Pre-Raphaelite group, and several of her poems appeared in their magazine *The Germ*. Her long, macabre poem *Goblin Market* (1862), a fairytale about forbidden pleasure, became extremely popular and was read to children. People generally seemed unaware of its buried sensuality, and would be shocked at the way modern readers have found in it themes relating to sex and virginity! Christina Rossetti never married, was sincerely devout, and much of her poetry is religious.

Church and religion were very important in Victorian times. Many people were religious and were devoted to helping those less fortunate. The issue of slavery aroused great sympathy, particularly among women, some of whom felt a link between the slaves' position and their own. In 1831 an anti-slavery group published the autobiography of a Bermudan woman slave who had managed to escape. Called *The History of Mary Prince, A West Indian Slave*, it described such horrific cruelty that there was a public outcry.

The most influential book on the subject was *Uncle Tom's Cabin* (1852), a novel by the American Harriet Beecher Stowe (1811–96). It played a part in bringing about the American Civil War and an end to slavery. When President Lincoln received Mrs Stowe at the White House, he apparently exclaimed: 'Is this the little woman who made this great war?' British women writers were very impressed by her. Charlotte Brontë said 'I voluntarily and sincerely veil my face before such a mighty subject as that handled in Mrs Beecher Stowe's work . . .'

Right A newspaper notice advertising the sale of slaves. The issue of slavery became very important in the 1830s, and many women wrote about the subject.

Harriet Martineau (1802–76)

Harriet Martineau was the daughter of a Norwich wool merchant, a sickly child who was born with no sense of smell or taste. At twelve she went deaf and had to use an ear trumpet (an old-fashioned hearing aid), but managed to complete her schooling. She became engaged to be married, but her fiancé became mentally ill, so she chose to remain at home with her parents instead. When her father died she took in sewing to help support the family and began publishing anonymous political articles, working early in the morning and late at night so as to appear suitably idle and 'ladylike' to visitors. Eventually her work paid so well that she began writing openly.

'I want to do something with the pen, since no other means of action in politics are in a woman's power,' she wrote. Through journalism she educated the British nation in the facts of industry, labour and trade. She regularly wrote leading editorial articles in the *Daily News*. In her famous *Illustrations of Political Economy* (1832–4) she explained economic ideas clearly through stories. The *Illustrations* earned her more than £2,000, whereas she had received a mere £15 a year on the *Daily News*.

In 1834 Harriet Martineau visited America and wrote *Society in America*, in which she made an important connection between the position of women and that of slaves. She was a great friend of Florence Nightingale, and helped publicize her ideas for reform. She was sensitive to harsh male criticism of her outspoken views, and did not always feel strong enough to accept new challenges. In 1837 she was offered the editorship of a new economics journal, but declined — and set about the more 'acceptable' task of writing a novel, *Deerbrook* (1839).

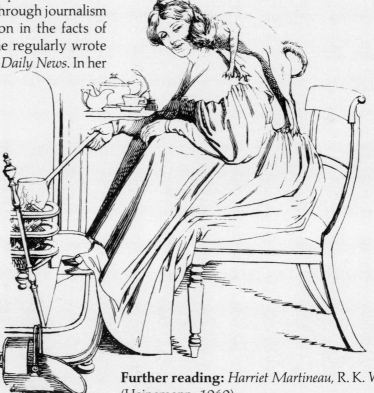

An informal picture of Harriet Martineau, who supported herself and her family by writing.

Further reading: *Harriet Martineau*, R. K. Webb (Heinemann, 1960).

Above During the second half of the nineteenth century, women still spent a great deal of time at home. There were many books and magazines about cooking and entertaining; one of the most famous was Mrs Beeton's The Book of Household Management.

6

Entertainment and Escapism

1850-1900

Literature gradually became a respectable and reasonably well-paid profession for women. Certain circulating libraries specialized in novels by women: some male authors complained about the female competition, as they found it more difficult to get their work published! Between the 1840s and 1880s the proportion of women published by Bentleys increased from 20 per cent to 40 per cent. Payment also improved: the fee for a first novel could equal a governess's annual wage. Once published, a writer could then get journalistic work, for which pay trebled during the second half of the century.

At the same time, however, women's horizons were being narrowed. The Victorians idealized family life and expected women to be devoted to the home – not to intellectual or public issues. Magazines for women began to stress fashion and cookery, leaving news and politics to men. As early as 1825 the editor of *The Lady's Magazine* complained that times had changed: women 'now seek only to exercise their virtues in domestic retirement'. He also noted that journals and reviews were full of sarcastic comments about intellectual women.

In 1852 Samuel Beeton published the first cheap monthly magazine for middle-class women, *The Englishwoman's Domestic Magazine*. It

Right An illustration from Mrs Beeton's The Book of Household Management *showing how a table for lunch should be laid!*

cost twopence — a sixth of the usual price for a magazine — and by 1860 its circulation was 50,000. It concentrated on home interests. His wife, Isabella Beeton (1836–65), contributed articles on cookery and fashion, 'Cupid's Letter Bag' gave advice on love, there was serial fiction and poetry, and sections on gardening, pets, hygiene and home nursing. Mrs Beeton later edited the magazine herself, and became famous for *The Book of Household Management* (1861), which covered all aspects of housewifery: management of servants, the arts of the hostess, accounts — and of course cookery.

As yet there were no special magazines for working-class women. They worked long hours in factories, fields or coal mines and did their own housework when they returned home. There was little time for reading. They were badly paid and could only afford 'penny dreadfuls', which were full of bloodthirsty crime stories.

From the 1850s there was a spate of best-selling novels by women. To start with these were very moral and suitable for reading aloud to the family. Charlotte Yonge (1823–1901), came from a fervently Christian family who agreed that she should give all her profits from writing to local church funds. Her most famous novel, *The Heir of Redclyffe* (1853), had a religious message and appealed to a wide readership — from young ladies at home to soldiers fighting in the Crimean war. Another 'moral' author, Dinah Craik (1826–88), felt writing was a divine mission. Her best-seller *John Halifax, Gentleman*

> *Do not gloss over faults or carelessness, and never allow one day's work to be left for the next ... Be firm, strict, yet kind and thoughtful to your servants, and they should respect you and carry out your wishes.* Isabella Beeton, *The Book of Household Management*, 1861.

Below left *Reading aloud was a popular family pastime in the Victorian era.*

Below *Charlotte Yonge. Her religious, moralistic novels were suitable for the whole family.*

WONDERFUL ADVENTURES of MRS SEACOLE

LONDON
JAMES BLACKWOOD
PATERNOSTER ROW

The front cover of Mary Seacole's Wonderful Adventures.

(1857) was a rags-to-riches story with a model hero. It appealed to the Victorian public because it stressed the value of religion and hard work.

During the 1860s female authors began writing 'sensation' novels, using melodramatic themes such as murder, double identity, mystery and escape. A disapproving reviewer sneered that they brought the reading matter of the kitchen (i.e. 'penny dreadfuls') into the drawing room. Mary E. Braddon (1835–1915) was so successful at this sort of writing that she was called the 'Queen of the circulating libraries'. She wrote over eighty books and was admired by famous writers including Tennyson. Her first great success, *Lady Audley's Secret* (1862), is a compelling detective story about a young woman who marries for money, hiding a previous marriage. Many reviewers were disturbed by the heroine, an innocent-looking blonde who carries out her crimes in high society single-handedly. They saw her as a threat to their ideal of the meek, dependent woman.

'Sensation' novelists had passionate and bold heroines and gradually they wrote more openly about sex. Rhoda Broughton (1840–1920) introduced kissing in her love scenes. Geraldine Jewsbury [see Chapter 5] tried to stop Bentleys publishing house from taking on Broughton's early novels because of their tone and explicit nature. Novels by Marie Corelli (1864–1924) were so daring that they had to be hidden from children. Many 'sensation' novels had heroines who ran away, or 'happy' endings with the death of a cruel husband. This undermined the rosy picture of respectable Victorian family life!

Not all best-sellers were fictional. During the severe winter of 1854–5 there was a public outcry about the appalling conditions of soldiers fighting in the Crimea. Food, medicine and clothing there were in short supply; hospitals were cess-pits of vermin and infection; and there were serious epidemics of disease. While Florence Nightingale worked in the military hospital, Mary Seacole (1805–81), a Jamaican woman of mixed racial origin, set up as a nurse and hotel-owner. She returned to Britain as a 'Crimean heroine' and her book, *Wonderful Adventures of Mrs Seacole in Many Lands* (1857), was an instant success. As well as describing the Crimea, she wrote about her childhood in Jamaica and travels in Central America.

Travel books were an important form of escapism. Several extraordinary Victorian women explored wild, unknown regions and wrote accounts of their adventures. Isabella Bird Bishop (1831–1904) was the most famous, and wrote books with exotic titles, such as *Unbeaten Tracks in Japan* (1890) and *The Yangtze Valley and Beyond*. By a strange contradiction she had poor health in Britain but amazing stamina when exploring far-flung places – 'the invalid at home and the Samson abroad' said her confused doctor. Perhaps it was the restriction of home life that made her ill.

7

The Woman Question

1860-1920

Throughout the second half of the nineteenth century people began to argue fiercely about women's rights. 'The Woman Question' focused on whether women should have 'suffrage' – the vote – and the 'suffragettes' campaigned hard to achieve this. They finally succeeded in 1918, when the vote was given to women over 30. In 1928 women received the vote at 21, on the same terms as men.

Before the question of suffrage came to a head, women began fighting for other important rights. They felt they should have a better education and be allowed to work in more professions. Emily Davies (1830–1921) argued for equal education and helped to found the first women's university college, Girton College, Cambridge, in

Above *In the late nineteenth century, women campaigned fiercely for the vote. This anti-suffrage postcard shows some men's solution for silencing women.*

Below *Stanley Library, Girton College, Cambridge in 1900.*

> **Why have women passion, intellect, moral activity – these three – and a place in society where no one of these three can be exercized?** Florence Nightingale, *Cassandra*, 1851.

> *... it is unjust to punish the sex who are the victims of a vice, and leave unpunished the sex who are the main cause ...* Josephine Butler, *Daily News*, 1870.

> **All men whose opinion is worth having prefer the simple and genuine girl of the past, with her tender little ways and pretty, bashful modesties, to this loud and rampant modernization, with her false red hair and painted skin, talking slang as glibly as a man, and by preference leading the conversation to doubtful subjects.** Elizabeth Lynn Linton, a well-known novelist, *The Saturday Review*, 1868.

1869. Florence Nightingale (1820–1910) expressed her anger at the way upper-class women were expected to be idle in her essay *Cassandra* (1851). She helped to make nursing a respectable profession, and her book *Notes on Nursing* (1861) revolutionized hospital management.

Journalism was important in publicizing women's ideas. In 1869 Emily Faithfull (1835–95) founded the Victoria Printing Press, which had an all-female staff and trained women in the printing trades. It published several suffragette journals, including *Women's Suffrage Journal*, edited by Lydia Becker, and the *English Woman's Journal*, which had been founded by Barbara Bodichon in 1858. These two women were important campaigners. Emma Patterson, the women's union organizer, founded the Women's Printing Society and edited the *Women's Union Journal* until her death.

Another important campaign concerned sex, a subject which ladies were not supposed to discuss. From the time of the Crimean War, when soldiers commonly visited prostitutes, there was a bad outbreak of sexually transmitted diseases, known as 'venereal' diseases. In 1864 the government passed the first of the Contagious Diseases Acts to control the epidemic. Suspected prostitutes were physically examined, often roughly, by doctors to see if they were infected, and could be imprisoned for anything up to nine months. Josephine Butler (1828–1906) argued that it was unfair for prositututes to be locked up and punished. In 1870 an article in the *Daily News* demanding abolition of the Acts was signed by 124 famous women, including Florence Nightingale and Harriet Martineau.

In 1877 Annie Besant (1847–1933) and Charles Bradlaugh published a pamphlet about contraception. They were accused of obscenity and their famous trial was an important test of freedom in publishing. A lot of people thought birth control was sinful: one newspaper said that 'no poison, moral or material, was ever offered to mankind so evil as this philosophy'. What is more, the court decided Annie Besant (who was divorced) was unfit to look after her young daughter, who was taken away.

Many people, including women, disapproved of those who campaigned for women's rights. They felt the 'New Woman' was immodest and unattractive. There were debates in the newspapers, but male editors of women's popular magazines carefully avoided the issue, afraid of upsetting their readers and losing sales.

In 1903 Emmeline and Christabel Pankhurst founded their own suffrage party, the Women's Social and Political Union, in an effort to gain the vote for women. In 1908 Elizabeth Robins (1862–1952) became president of the Women Writers' Suffrage League, bringing professional authors together to influence public opinion. Her own play, *Votes for Women!* (1907), which she turned into a novel called

from the COMEDY THEATRE LONDON

IN HONOUR AND IN LOVING, REVERENT MEMORY OF
EMILY WILDING DAVISON.

The Convert, was a famous piece of propaganda for the movement. It gives a picture of how it felt to be a suffragette, and most of its second act is taken up by a suffrage meeting in Trafalgar Square. The heroine blackmails an MP, her former lover, threatening to convert his fiancée to the women's movement if he does not support the suffrage bill!

One of the founders of the Women Writers' Suffrage League was Cicely Hamilton (1872–1952), who wrote *Marriage as a Trade* (1909), an important analysis of women's economic dependence on men. Like Elizabeth Robins she was an actress, and wrote several plays. Her comedy about a women's general strike, *How the Vote was Won*, was first performed in 1909. In the same year the famous actress Ellen Terry starred in her play *A Pageant of Great Women*, which was a history of great female artists, rulers, saints and warriors.

As women marched for a common cause 'shoulder to shoulder and friend to friend', class barriers began to break down. Working-class women made a valuable contribution to the suffrage struggle, although many women had little time to do anything other than work, sew, clean and care for children. The remarkable and invaluable diaries of Hannah Cullwick give a detailed account of the life of an ordinary working-class woman and her work in domestic service.

Above left A poster advertising a play, The New Woman. *It made fun of women who were too 'bookish' and independent.*

Above right Women published many magazines to publicize the suffrage cause. The Suffragette *magazine was edited by Christabel Pankhurst. This edition reports the death of Emily Wilding Davison who ran in front of King George V's horse at the Derby in 1913, to protest about the conditions faced by suffragettes in prison.*

Hannah Cullwick (1833–1909)

Hannah Cullwick was born in Shropshire, the daughter of a housemaid and a saddler. She learned to read and write at a charity school and began work in domestic service at the age of eight. During her life she worked in many households, usually doing the heaviest kind of domestic work.

In 1854 she met Arthur Munby, an eccentric upper-class gentleman who was fascinated by lower-class women. They became 'sweethearts' and eventually married in 1873 – all in total secret, as they came from different classes. During their eighteen-year courtship Hannah Cullwick kept detailed diaries for Munby, who wanted a full record of her daily life and work. Her writing had to be secret, which was difficult as servants had little privacy. Work dominated her life: the seventeen diaries describe her daily tasks, constant changes of situation, and relationships with employers and fellow servants. She was very strong and a hard worker and felt that 'for freedom and true lowliness there's nothing like being a maid of all work. No one can think you set up or proud'.

When she married she stopped writing for Munby; she did not particularly enjoy the task. She stopped living with him after four years, refusing to act the gentlewoman and preferring independence. Her diaries were not published until 1984.

Further reading: *The Diaries of Hannah Cullwick*, ed. Liz Stanley (Virago, 1984).

> *Miss K. thought me very strong, and so I am, 4 times stronger nor she is I should say, for she could not sew well either, therefore a poor drudge like me is more use in a lodging house than her being a brought-up lady, as couldn't boil a 'tatoe [potato] when she first came . . .* Hannah Cullwick's diaries, 1866–72.

Right *Hannah Cullwick, a Victorian maidservant, gives us an important glimpse of the hard life of working-class women in her detailed diaries.*

8

The Legacy of Wars
1920-1950

In 1920 several women who had been suffragettes founded a successful women's weekly magazine, *Time and Tide* — named after the popular saying 'Time and tide wait for no man'. Its first editorial said that 'as newcomers to the political game' women needed a magazine that reported the effect of national and foreign news on women. Important contributors included Elizabeth Robins and Cicely Hamilton [see previous chapter], Rebecca West, Winifred Holtby and Vera Brittain.

The journalist and novelist Winifred Holtby (1898–1935) fought for women's rights and peace, but died young. During the First World War (1914–18) she served in France in the Women's Auxiliary Army Corps. At Oxford University she became close friends with Vera Brittain, who later wrote a book about her, *Testament of Friendship* (1940). As well as contributing to *Time and Tide*, Winifred Holtby wrote regularly in several daily newspapers and in *Good Housekeeping*, and was considered the finest journalist in London. Her best-known novel *South Riding* (1936), a portrait of life in Yorkshire, was published after her death and won a literary prize.

Her friend Vera Brittain (1893–1970) served as a nurse during the First World War and wrote a famous book about her experiences, *Testament of Youth* (1933). She had become a convinced pacifist and wanted 'to show that war was not glamour or glory but abysmal grief and purposeless waste'. During the Second World War she outraged the British public by criticizing the heavy Allied bombing of German cities and wrote a pamphlet called *Massacre by Bombing*. Even in her seventies she joined in demonstrations organized by the Campaign for Nuclear Disarmament.

Some writers responded to the horrors of war by turning inward. Dorothy Richardson (1873–1957) devoted her life to a twelve-volume work about a woman's experiences: *Pilgrimage* (1915–38). She pioneered in England a style known as 'stream of consciousness', which follows thoughts and impressions rather than a structured story. James Joyce also used this technique in *Ulysses* (1922), and *Pilgrimage* has often been overshadowed and neglected in comparison. Dorothy Richardson herself disliked the term 'stream of consciousness',

Vera Brittain as a nurse in the First World War. Her book Testament of Youth *describes her horrific experiences during the war.*

‘ **The enemy within shelling distance — refugee Sisters crowding in with nerves all awry — bright moonlight, and aeroplanes carrying machine guns — ambulance trains jolting noisily into the sidings, all day, all night — gassed men on stretchers, clawing the air — dying men, reeking with mud and foul green-stained bandages, shrieking and writhing in a grotesque travesty of manhood — dead men with fixed, empty eyes and shiny yellow faces . . .** Vera Brittain, *Testament of Youth*, 1933. **’**

The eccentric poet and writer Edith
Sitwell. She often based her poetry
on musical forms.

preferring to describe the style as 'dramatic monologue'. Both she
and Virginia Woolf saw the technique as trying to create a female
writing form and a female language.

The early twentieth century was a time of experimentation with
form and language. The American writer Gertrude Stein (1874–1946)
wrote poems, essays, plays and novels in an unusual style, playing
with words and repetitive phrases. She lived in Paris, a close friend
of Picasso and other Cubist painters, and wanted to use their artistic
ideas in her writing. Edith Sitwell (1888–1964) also shocked people
with a poetic style based on musical forms. Her *Façade* poems were
set to music by William Walton; they caused a sensation when first
performed in 1923. Later she was hailed as an original writer and
was given many prizes and honorary degrees.

The most important, brilliant, experimental female writer was
Virginia Woolf (1882–1941). She used dazzling poetical prose to
describe the physical world and to explore her characters' inner lives.
Together with her husband Leonard, she started The Hogarth Press

6
very fine is my valentine
very fine and very mine
very mine is my valentine very
mine and very fine
very fine is my valentine and
mine, very fine very fine and
mine is my valentine
Gertrude Stein, *Collected Poems*,
1946.
9

in 1917, and published small editions of work they valued. Her novels won her fame, but she suffered from a series of mental breakdowns and eventually committed suicide. In *Mrs Dalloway* (1925) she expressed madness through the mind of a shell-shocked soldier, whose disturbed ideas jar against the thoughts and memories of the heroine. Virginia Woolf was a highly respected critic and wrote regularly for the *Times Literary Supplement*. Her famous book *A Room of One's Own* (published from earlier lectures in 1929) forms the basis of many modern theories about women and literature [see Chapter 1].

Virginia Woolf's friend Vita Sackville-West (1892–1962) was also a well-known novelist and poet. Her novel *All Passion Spent* (1931) echoes *A Room of One's Own* as a plea for every woman's right to 'simply be herself'. The heroine, the newly-widowed Lady Slane, spends her last years alone, quietly 'looking back on the girl she had once been'. Vita Sackville-West received a great many letters from women who felt that, like Lady Slane, they had sacrificed their lives to their husbands and children.

> *Now the sun had sunk. Sky and sea were indistinguishable. The waves breaking spread their white fans far out over the shore, sent white shadows into the recesses of sonorous caves and then rolled back sighing over the shingle.* Virginia Woolf, *The Waves*, 1931.

The Hogarth Press motif. Virginia and her husband, Leonard Woolf, set up this small publishing company to print works they valued. Much of the printing was done by hand.

> *[The woman writer] will find that she is perpetually wishing to alter the established values — to make serious what appears insignificant to man, and trivial what is to him important.* Virginia Woolf, *Women and Fiction*, 1929.

Virginia Woolf as a young woman. She was a very original novelist, and is now well respected for her views on women and writing.

Above Front cover of Home Making
magazine in 1933.

Above Front cover of a Mills & Boon
romantic novel in 1939. These novels
were very popular during the Depression.

Some women excelled at writing short stories. The New Zealander Katherine Mansfield (1888–1923) made her name with sensitive, perceptive stories – some funny, some sad, many with the theme of betrayal. Unfortunately, she died young. Jean Rhys (1890–1979) wrote novels and short stories about women as underdogs, unable to control their fate and heartlessly exploited by men.

Many novelists focused on the theme of personal relationships. Rosamond Lehmann (b. 1901) had a genius for evoking the emotional atmosphere of a period. Throughout her long career her novels have reflected the changing problems encountered by women. When her first book *Dusty Answer* was published in 1927, she received hundreds of letters from women who felt she had told their own unhappy love story. Antonia White (1899–1980) made her name with an autobiographical novel, *Frost in May* (1933), which was a portrait of a child's life in a Catholic convent, and three novels formed its sequel. She also translated many works by the French novelist Colette (1873–1954), another important figure. Colette is most famous for *Cheri* (1920), the story of an older woman's love for a young man who lives off her money. Her work celebrates women's sexuality, wisdom and power.

Although many great women writers were active during the first part of this century, not all were popular or even well known. Some were difficult to understand, and many were not writing for the mass market. Often they had discouraging reviews from critics who were not interested in 'the female experience'. It has taken time for their contribution to be recognized.

During the 1930s Depression, the publishing company Mills & Boon began to have great success with romantic novels in twopenny libraries. These catered for women, and were written by women – or men with female pseudonyms. They provided light entertainment and escapism, with simple stories leading to an inevitable happy ending: 'true' love and marriage. During the Second World War, they began featuring wounded heroes, and 'hospital' romances also became very popular.

The market in women's magazines changed greatly. After the First World War, 'society' journals were replaced by new publications for middle- and lower-class women. In the 1930s–1940s new colour printing techniques made it possible to produce mass circulation magazines such as *Woman's Own* and *Home Making* magazine. Women began to be influenced by advertisers, who used persuasive methods to encourage them to buy beauty or domestic products. During the Second World War women took over many 'men's' jobs, but when peace came they were expected to return to being housewives. Women's magazines stressed old-fashioned values and told them it was best to stay at home.

Rebecca West (1892–1983)

Rebecca West was born in London as Cicily Fairfield, the daughter of an army officer. Her writing career started at the age of fourteen when she published an article about women's suffrage in *The Scotsman* newspaper. She adopted the pseudonym 'Rebecca West' after playing the strong-willed heroine of that name in a play by the Norwegian playwright Ibsen. At nineteen, she worked as a journalist for the feminist magazine *Freewoman*, and later on the socialist paper *Clarion*. By 1920, when *Time and Tide* began, she was a famous journalist, well known for her socialist and feminist views.

Rebecca West's range is considerable: she was a remarkable journalist, a fine novelist, and an excellent critic. Her collected essays *The Strange Necessity* (1928) are similar in stature to those of Virginia Woolf. In *Henry James* (1916) she highlighted Henry James' stereotyped portrayal of women: it is the first example of modern 'feminist' literary criticism. Her first novel, *The Return of the Soldier*, about a shell-shocked soldier, was published in 1918, and has now become a film. *The Judge* (1922) raised issues which had previously been thought too shocking to discuss: rape and unmarried motherhood. It coincided with the end of West's long love affair with the writer H. G. Wells, the father of their illegitimate son born in 1914. Later novels are about the 'Aubrey' family during the first

Rebecca West as a young woman. She started publishing her writing at the age of fourteen.

half of the century, the best-known being *The Fountain Overflows* (1957).

All her life Rebecca West was committed to feminism and social reform. In 1937 she published *Black Lamb and Grey Falcon*, a two-volume book about a trip to the Balkans which is a study of European history and the inevitable coming of the Second World War. She was honoured by being made a Dame Commander, Order of the British Empire in 1959, and continued to travel widely and write until her death at the age of ninety.

> **I myself have never been able to find out precisely what feminism is; I only know that people call me a feminist whenever I express sentiments that differentiate me from a doormat . . .** Rebecca West, 1913.

Further reading: *Rebecca West: A Life*, Victoria Glendinning (Weidenfeld and Nicolson, 1987).

The first edition of the feminist magazine Spare Rib in 1972.

But now, sitting with Molly talking, as they had so many hundreds of times before, Anna was saying to herself: Why do I always have this awful need to make other people see things as I do? It's childish, why should they? What it amounts to is that I'm scared of being alone in what I feel. Doris Lessing, *The Golden Notebook*, 1962.

... the image of an attractive woman is the most effective advertising gimmick. She may sit astride the mudguard of a new car ... she may lie at a man's feet stroking his new socks ... whatever she does her image sells. Germaine Greer, *The Female Eunuch*, 1970.

9

The Feminist Revival

1950 onwards

After the Second World War, women were expected to return to the role of housewife, leaving power in the hands of men. During the 1950s more opportunities arose for women to take jobs outside the home, often as a result of advances in technology, and this created a change of social climate. By the 1960s women began to protest about their inferior position in society. After all, women made up a third of the nation's labour force but on average were paid only three-quarters of the male wage.

The first important book for 'women's liberation' was *The Second Sex* (1949) by the French writer Simone de Beauvoir (1908–86). She pointed out that men set the standards, and women were always made to feel 'second best'. In *The Feminine Mystique* (1963) the American journalist Betty Friedan challenged the idea that all women were happy as housewives. She interviewed women in the USA and found that, although many thought they were happy, some were being treated by psychoanalysts or taking tranquillizers. Many suffered from depression.

Novelists and poets began writing about women's struggle for more control over their own lives. Doris Lessing's novel *The Golden Notebook* (1962) captured modern women's feelings of confusion and anger and was very important to those in the 'liberation movement'. Similarly, American-born Sylvia Plath (1932–63) wrote highly personal poems about her situation as a woman. She married the poet Ted Hughes and had two children, but became very depressed because she had no time to herself. In fact, she had to get up very early in the morning in order to find enough peacefulness to write. Eventually she committed suicide. *Ariel* (1965) is her most famous collection of poetry. Her powerful novel about mental illness, *The Bell Jar* was published in the year of her death.

In 1970 an Australian lecturer in English, Germaine Greer, published *The Female Eunuch*, a book that caused quite a sensation. In it she tried to show how women have been conditioned to be dominated by men. She demonstrated that the beauty industry, magazines and romantic fiction have created 'love' and 'marriage' as an idealized trap, so that women's own illusions about love place them in men's power. Amid much hostile publicity she called on women to fight for change and freedom.

The monthly magazine *Spare Rib* was founded in 1972 by a group of journalists whose original idea was simply to produce a magazine for women by women. It became important for its discussion of women's issues and developed an increasingly strong commitment to feminism. In the same year *Cosmopolitan* magazine, a glossy American monthly, was successfully launched in Britain. It appealed to ambitious 'professional' women and placed great emphasis on glamour and sex issues. Both magazines are still available today. Although they are very different, together they reflect the impact of the feminist revival: greater awareness of injustice towards women, along with improved expectations and career prospects.

In the same year – 1972 – the Virago Press publishing company was founded by the Australian Carmen Callil. Its aim was (and still is) to publish books which 'illuminate and celebrate all aspects of women's lives'. Virago – which means 'heroic woman' – wanted to establish a new, positive image of womanhood.

Virago publishes modern fiction and non-fiction, but became particularly famous for its 'Modern Classics' series. This reprints novels by nineteenth and early twentieth-century writers, and much valuable work has come to light. Writers such as Antonia White, Rosamond

The walls were bright, white lavatory tile with bald bulbs set at intervals in a black ceiling. Stretchers and wheelchairs were beached here and there against the hissing, knocking pipes that ran and branched in an intricate nervous system along the glittering walls. I hung on to Doctor Nolan's arm like death, and every so often she gave me an encouraging squeeze. Finally, we stopped at a green door with Electrotherapy printed on it in black letters... Sylvia Plath, *The Bell Jar*, 1963.

Virago Press's Modern Classics series has been important in bringing to light the work of women authors of the past.

Lehmann, Rebecca West and Dorothy Richardson [see Chapter 8] are the most important examples. Antonia White was reprinted after twenty years' silence – shortly before her death – and her work has become extremely popular. When Rosamond Lehmann was republished after an equally long time, she made a speech at Virago quoting from the Bible: 'I know that my Redeemer [saviour] liveth'!

The 'Virago Travellers' series reprints work by past travel writers such as Isabella Bird Bishop [see Chapter 6]. There is also an extensive list of non-fictional classics by authors such as Rebecca West and Harriet Martineau.

Another important idea at Virago has been to discover 'the hidden voices of ordinary women'. Many fascinating writers have been published for the first time. *The Hard Way Up*, the secret autobiography of Hannah Mitchell, a working class suffragette, was published in 1977. The diaries of the Victorian maidservant Hannah Cullwick [see Chapter 7] have also been published.

The Women's Press is another important women's publishing company. It began in 1977, operating from its founder Stephanie Dowrick's East London front room, and has since flourished and grown. Its slogan 'live authors, live issues' emphasizes up-to-date work, both fiction and non-fiction.

In 1985 The Women's Press launched a science fiction series, bringing a new approach to this type of imaginative writing. The classics of science fiction come from America: *The Female Man* by Joanna Russ, *Woman on the Edge of Time* by Marge Piercy, and *The Wanderground* by Sally Miller Gearhart. These books all challenge and question human society as organized by men.

Thanks to these and other publishers, we can now read a growing

The Women's Press concentrates on the work of modern feminist writers and has encouraged many new writers to seek publication, including Millie Murray and Joan Riley. They have also published Alice Walker's famous novel The Color Purple.

body of fictional work by women. One of the most highly regarded authors is Zoë Fairbairns, whose political novels *Benefits*, *Here Today* and *Closing* are set in modern London. Another is Michèle Roberts, a poet who has written several novels on themes relating to mythology and self-knowledge. *The Wild Girl* is an imaginary fifth Gospel according to Mary Magdalene, looking at the message of Christianity from a feminist point of view.

At first the feminist movement was mainly concerned with the problems of Western women. More recently women began to realize that this viewpoint was rather narrow and that they could learn from the experience of women from ethnic minorities and developing nations. Several black American writers have become well known, in particular Alice Walker and Maya Angelou, the great successes of recent publishing history. Alice Walker's most famous novel *The Color Purple* won the Pulitzer prize. It is set in the American Deep South and written in the Black American dialect. Maya Angelou has written vivid autobiographies; the first was *I Know Why the Caged Bird Sings*.

Important non-Western writers include the Egyptian Nawal El Saadawi, who has written several books and novels on women in the Arab world, and Suniti Namjoshi, an Indian poet and story-teller. Although not feminist in outlook, Anita Desai has become famous for her sensitive, observant accounts of life in Indian villages and cities and the conflict between tradition and change. She made her name with *Fire on the Mountain* (1978), which won prizes in Britain and India, and she has twice been short-listed for the Booker McConnell Prize. In Britain interesting work has come from Joan Riley, a novelist of Jamaican origin and Grace Nichols, a Guyanan-born poet whose book *The Fat Black Woman's Poems* challenges the Western stereotype of womanhood as slim, highly organized and competitive!

Many general publishers now have feminist sections, and the scope for women writers is continually widening. Feminist crime writers are becoming very popular. Books are also being produced for the teenage market. Women's handbooks exist on a variety of practical subjects. Much important work from the past is still being reprinted. Pandora Press has a 'Mothers of the Novel' series, reprinting work by early authors such as Charlotte Smith, Maria Edgeworth and Elizabeth Inchbald [see Chapter 4].

The impact of feminism on literature has been enormous. A new field – Women's Studies – looks at women's achievements in all aspects of life, as well as their oppression. The sociologist Ann Oakley and Australian-born historian Dale Spender have made a great contribution to the understanding of women's role in society. All in all, more women are choosing writing as a career, and many more are being read.

In her poems and autobiographical novels, Maya Angelou gives us a detailed picture of the life of a black American woman.

Doris Lessing (b. 1919)

Doris Tayler was born in Persia (now Iran) in 1919. Her family then went to live on a large farm in Southern Rhodesia (now Zimbabwe, but in those days a British colony). Doris was a difficult child, and left school at fourteen. Later she moved to the capital, Salisbury, married and had two children. In 1942 her marriage broke up. She joined a communist group, and in 1945 married its leader, a German named Lessing. Working for communist ideals was an important experience for Doris – it inspired her work, but later brought disillusionment.

In 1949, her second marriage ended and she came to London, bringing the manuscript of her first novel *The Grass is Singing* with her. It dealt with sensitive racial issues, describing a white woman's fear of and attraction to her black servant. When published in 1950 it was an international success.

In London, Lessing made friends with political exiles and worked for the communist movement, but in 1956 she left the party because of her disapproval of the Soviet invasion of Hungary. That year she was banned from South Africa and Southern Rhodesia for her criticism of the governments in those countries, who dominated black people and kept them powerless. She had already begun her famous sequence of novels about the character 'Martha Quest', whose experiences were based on Lessing's own life. The sequence of novels is called *The Children of Violence* (1952–69). We follow Martha's problems as a wife and mother, her involvement with communism, divorce and her move to London.

In 1962 Lessing published her most important novel, *The Golden Notebook*. The novel is divided into separate notebooks. The main character 'Anna', a 'free woman' without a husband, is a

Doris Lessing has tackled many themes in her writing, including racism, communism and feminism.

writer and communist who cracks under the strain of trying to mirror the effect of war, poverty and famine in her work. It became a feminist 'Bible', although the book covers a great many more issues.

The end of the *Children of Violence* sequence takes place in a bleak future, after some massive destruction on earth. In some ways, it marked Lessing's move away from realism. Later she began writing science fiction, and completed a five-volume epic called *Canopus in Argos: Archives* (1979–83). This gave Lessing more imaginative freedom, allowing her to work out her moral and political ideas on a large scale.

Lessing's work is wide-ranging, original, and always politically aware. She has published a great deal – novels, short stories and non-fiction. Recently she was short-listed for the Booker McConnell Prize with *The Good Terrorist* (1985), a convincing portrait of a group of political activists. She has won international acclaim and numerous honours, and continues to live and write in London.

Further reading: *Doris Lessing*, Lorna Sage (Methuen, 1983).

10

Conclusion

Margaret Drabble is one of the many important women writers of today.

As you will have seen, the position and reputation of women writers has greatly improved since the time of Katherine Philips and Aphra Behn. Although the old prejudices about women's writing are still being voiced – that it is 'trivial', 'sentimental' or 'narrow' in view-point – this century has produced many outstanding women writers in the English language. Despite the fact that publishing is still dominated by men, more women are being published than ever before.

Women have gained recognition in all fields of writing.

• The novel continues to be a very important form of female expression. Iris Murdoch's intellectually brilliant work has won

Left *Iris Murdoch, winner of the Booker McConnell Prize in 1978. Her novel,* The Bell, *was dramatized for television.*

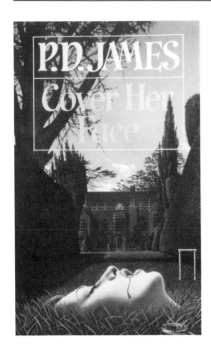

Above Front cover from one of P. D. James's crime mysteries.

numerous prizes, such as the 1974 Whitbread Literary Prize for *The Sacred and Profane Love Machine* and the 1978 Booker McConnell Prize for *The Sea, The Sea*. Other important novelists who have not already been mentioned include Ivy Compton-Burnett (1892–1969), Elizabeth Bowen (1899–1973), Muriel Spark, Penelope Lively, A. S. Byatt, Olivia Manning, Ruth Prawer Jhabvala, Angela Carter, Fay Weldon and Anita Brookner.

• Many women poets have become recognized. Stevie Smith (1902-71) had her first collection of poetry published in 1937 and won the Queen's Gold Medal for Poetry in 1969. Others are Elizabeth Jennings, Kathleen Raine and Patricia Beer.

• Women have earned an important place in the field of journalism, particularly for their serious treatment of social issues. Mary Stott edited the Women's Page of *The Guardian* newspaper from 1957–71, and her articles have been reprinted in book form. Other notable journalists are Katharine Whitehorn, Jill Tweedie, and Polly Toynbee. Female critics have also been important; for instance Hermione Lee, a university lecturer who writes for *The Observer* and edits and writes books about women writers.

• Women have continued the tradition of travel writing established by Victorians such as Isabella Bird Bishop. Freya Stark is famous for her accounts of the Middle East, and the Irishwoman Dervla Murphy is well known for her travels round the world on a bicycle.

• In science fiction the American Ursula Le Guin has become famous and won many awards. Other notable names in this field are Doris Lessing, Tanith Lee and Joanna Russ.

• Famous crime, mystery and detection writers include Dorothy L. Sayers (1893–1957), Agatha Christie (1890–1976) and more recently P. D. James.

These are the main areas of achievement. It would be impossible to mention all the other women who have made important contributions to English literature – editors, biographers, dramatists, children's writers and authors on a wide variety of non-fictional subjects.

The place of women in the literary world is well established, and today people are readier to respect and read serious women writers. For this we must thank the earlier writers studied in this book. Through their determination, brilliance and courage, women today can be published, read and appreciated for their worth.

Left The poet Stevie Smith, who won the Queen's Gold Medal for poetry. Women have established themselves in every field of literature, from science fiction and crime mysteries to journalism.

Projects

Collect several current women's magazines and study their contents. How much space is given to politics, science, religion, law, the arts, health, fashion, beauty, personal problems, etc? What do these magazines have in common and what distinguishes them? What kind of women are they aimed at?

Find a 'romantic' novel — by Barbara Cartland or Denise Robins. Read the story and then try to imagine what happens after the 'happy ending'. Write a summary of the couple's life together for the next twenty years.

Find an older woman — your grandmother, aunt or neighbour — who has time to sit and talk. With her help, write a section of an imaginary diary from some part of her life. Remember to include practical details about housework, shopping, cooking, clothes and prices.

Look for anthologies of poetry — in libraries, bookshops and private book collections. Make a chart listing the title, date and editor of each one, and note how many women poets are included. This should provide an interesting indication of the way editors, publishers and critics have chosen men's and women's work respectively.

Glossary

Abysmal Bottomless, very deep.

Activists People committed to political change, usually by unconventional means.

Anonymous Unnamed.

Aspersions Spreading evil rumours or gossip about someone.

Awry Twisted, disturbed.

Bane Destructive force.

Broadsheet Large sheet of paper printed on one side with news, ballads, etc. and sold in the streets.

Charity schools Schools for poor children, maintained by church or local funds.

Communist Committed to communism, a political philosophy founded by Karl Marx according to which private property is abolished: these ideas were especially developed in the Soviet Union.

Coquetry Flirtatious behaviour.

Cubist painters Painters belonging to an artistic movement which began in Paris early this century and sought to invent new forms of expression in painting.

Devout Pious, devoted to religion.

Disillusionment Becoming free of illusions or false ideas.

Disreputable Bringing disgrace, having a bad reputation.

Domestic service Working as a household servant.

Drudge A person who does slavish work.

Electrotherapy A treatment for mental illness using electric shocks.

Expectations Assumptions about what will happen, future prospects.

Explicit Clear, definite, outspoken.

Feminist Committed to improving the position of women.

Forbearance Avoiding, refraining from.

Honorary degree Special university degree given as an honour, without the usual examinations.

Ideal, idealized Imagined in a perfect form.

Illusions Taken in by false appearances.

Imagery Scenery or pictures used to illustrate meaning, especially in poetry.

Immodest Shameless, indecent.

Immoral Improper or wrong behaviour, especially sexual.

Indistinguishable Difficult to tell apart, seeming to be identical.

Injustice Unfair treatment in relation to the rights of a person or group.

Intellectual To have 'academic' knowledge or intelligence.

Ironical Using language that has an inner meaning, often for the purpose of ridicule.

Malice Spite; the will to harm.

Melodramatic Overacted or over-dramatized; sensational or sentimental.

Monologue Long speech by one person.

Moral, moralistic Someone who practises and teaches good conduct; a writer who teaches correct behaviour through a story.

Mystique Mysterious power.

Pacifist Committed to promoting peace.

Perceptively With insight and great awareness.

Philosophy Code of practice or way of thinking; study of ideas.

Prefaces Introductory sections of a book.

Prejudice A biased, unfair view, especially against a minority group.

'Professional' women Women holding responsible positions in any institution or business.

Pseudonym Pen-name.

Psychoanalysts Doctors who treat emotional problems by analyzing the 'unconscious' mind.

Puritans Religious and political party which ruled Britain in the mid-seventeenth century, enforcing strict morals and behaviour.

Realism Representation of things as they are, true to life.

Redeemer Person who comes to the rescue.

'Sensation' novelist Writer who relies on melodramatic, sensational plots in novels for the commercial market.

Sensuality Deriving pleasure from the bodily senses.

Serial fiction Fiction published in separate instalments.

Sonorous Having a full, rich sound.

Stereotyped Viewing people or things according to a fixed formula, rather than seeing them as they really are.

Strictures Criticisms, explanation of wrongs.

Tract Short essay, especially on a religious or political subject.

Trivial Unimportant, worthless.

Twopenny libraries Commercial libraries in which the weekly subscription was twopence (less than 1p).

Undeviating Not being diverted by temptation.

Vice Sinful habit, immoral conduct.

Vindication Defence of something threatened; proof or justification of a belief.

Woodcut prints Pictures printed from a flat block of carved wood (an old printing technique).

Books to Read

Editions of most of the books mentioned in the text are still easily available today. More recent ones often contain a useful introduction. If you want to know who publishes a certain title, go to your local library's reference department and ask for an up-to-date copy of 'Books in Print'. If you look up either the title of the book, or just the author's name, you will be able to find out who the publishers are. Then, ask at the information desk if they hold that book in stock, or if they can order it for you.

Other books of interest are listed below.

Anthologies of poetry

Adcock, Fleur (ed) *The Faber Book of Twentieth Century Women's Poetry* (Faber and Faber, 1987)

Bernikow, Louise (ed) *The World Split Open: Women Poets 1552–1950* (The Women's Press, 1984)

Reilly, Catherine (ed) *Scars upon my Heart* (Virago Press, 1981) (poetry of the First World War)

Reilly, Catherine (ed) *Chaos of the Night* (Virago Press, 1984) (poetry of the Second World War)

Scott, Diana (ed) *Bread and Roses* (Virago Press, 1982) (nineteenth and twentieth century poetry)

Anthologies of prose

Dinesen, Betzy (ed) *Rediscovery* (The Women's Press, 1981) (including work by Aphra Behn, Margaret Cavendish, Elizabeth Robins and Dorothy Richardson)

Green, Jen and Lefanu, Sarah (eds) *Despatches from the Frontiers of the Female Mind* (The Women's Press, 1986) (science fiction stories)

Lee, Hermione (ed) *The Secret Self: Short Stories by Women* (vols 1 & 2) (J. M. Dent, 1985, 1988)

Spender, Dale (ed) *Time and Tide Wait for no Man* (Pandora Press, 1984) (reprinted from *Time and Tide*)

Stott, Mary (ed) *Women Talking: An Anthology from The Guardian Women's Page 1922–35 – 1957–71* (Pandora Press, 1987)

Drama

Considine, Ann and Slovo, Robyn (eds) *Dead Proud: From Second Wave Young Women Playwrights* (The Women's Press, 1987) (short one-act pieces from a London theatre project)

Morgan, Fidelis, *The Female Wits: Women Playwrights on the London Stage 1660–1720* (Virago Press, 1981) (includes plays by Aphra Behn and Mary de la Rivière Manley)

Biography and history for younger readers

Bennett, Olivia, *The Changing Status of Women* (Bell & Hyman, 1987)

Gatti, Anne, *Isabella Bird Bishop* (Hamish Hamilton, 1988)

Martin, Christopher, *The Brontës* (Wayland, 1988)

Warnock, Kitty, *Mary Wollstonecraft* (Hamish Hamilton, 1988)

Williams, Susan, *Jane Austen* (Wayland, 1988)

History and criticism for older readers

Adburgham, Alison, *Women in Print* (George Allen & Unwin, 1972)

Hanscombe, Gillian and Smyers, Virginia S., *Writing for Their Lives: The Modernist Woman, 1900–1940* (The Women's Press, 1987)

Moers, Ellen, *Literary Women* (The Women's Press, 1978)

Showalter, Elaine, *A Literature of Their Own* (Virago Press, 1978)

Spencer, Jane, *The Rise of the Woman Novelist from Aphra Behn to Jane Austen* (Basil Blackwell, 1986)

Spender, Dale, *Mothers of the Novel* (Pandora Press, 1986)

Swindells, Julia, *Victorian Writing and Working Women* (Polity Press, 1985)

Williams, Merryn, *Six Women Novelists* (Macmillan, 1987)

Winship, Janice, *Inside Women's Magazines* (Pandora Press, 1987)

Woolf, Virginia, *Women and Writing* (The Women's Press, 1979)

Index

Numbers that are printed in **bold** indicate illustrations.